SATISH GUJRAL

Sculptures

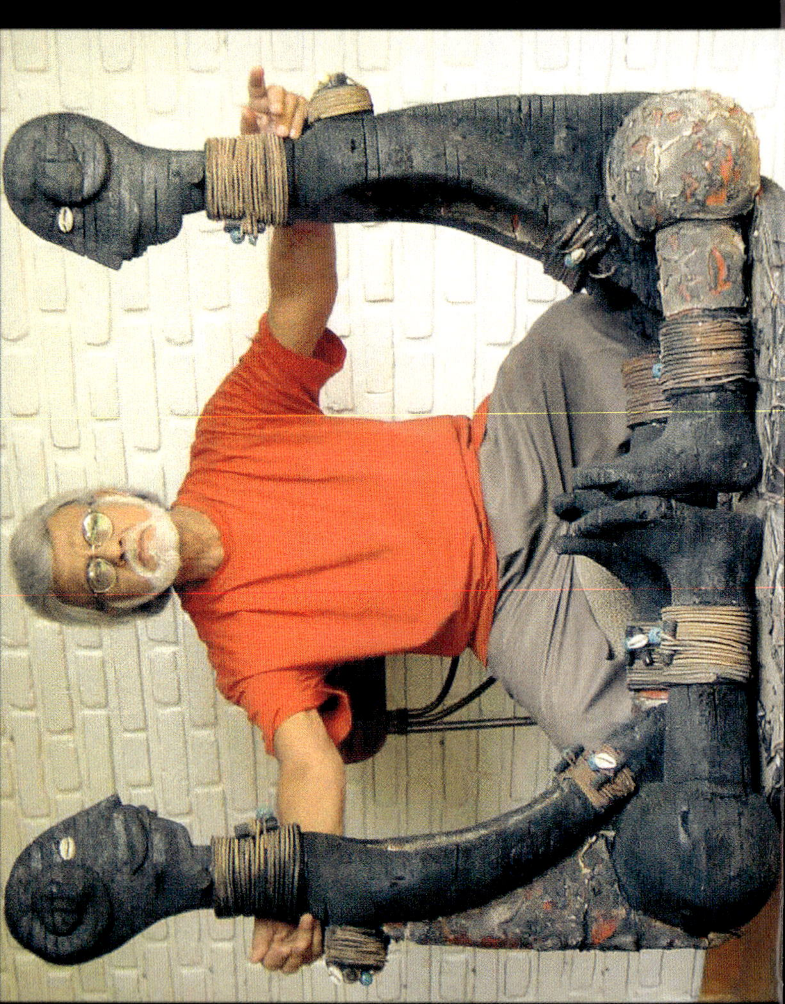

SATISH GUJRAL

Sculptures

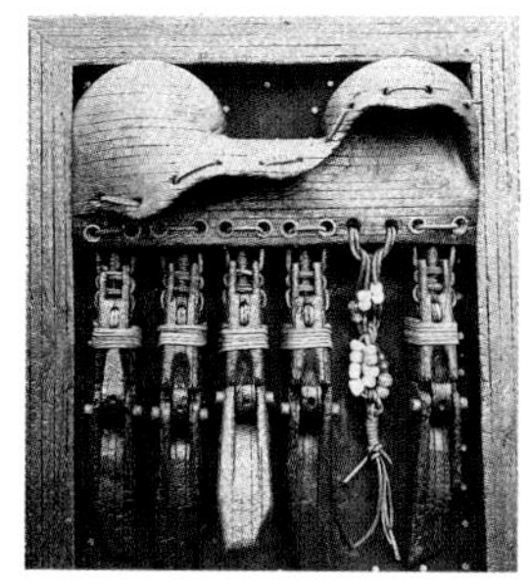

Satish Gujral

Lustre Press
Roli Books

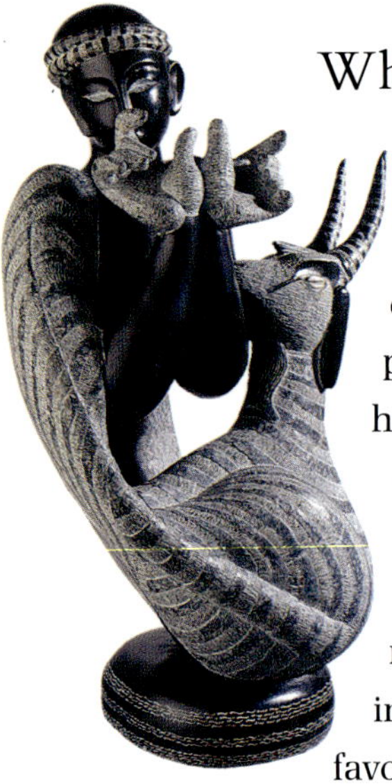

Whatever the medium, art, for me, is an expression of the adventures and discoveries of mankind as it reacts to an environment that demands perpetual readjustment between habit and the process of changing facts.

Creativity, being an expression of freedom and originality, knows no boundaries except those inherent within itself. It claims no favourites among styles or 'isms'. It is a timeless gauge for the art of ancient, modern, or future times. This includes all significant, creative, and more or less unified, human expressions of the material and spiritual world in which we believe.

I believe no expression is art unless it is creative.

Man and his pet, 28" ht., granite, 1998

To create is to select or invent elements significant to a given purpose and organise them into a new and unique form. It means originality. It means individuality. It means freedom of action. Creativity depends on a certain attitude of mind. It is an invitation to free thinking, exploration, and progression. Its opposite is imitation that spells conformity, reaction, and decadence.

An artist, to my mind, has objectives: he attempts to reproduce the outer and/or inner meaning of the appearance of things – using individually conceived forms that are the products of his experience, feeling, or imagination – to express his aesthetic ideas and emotions in the medium employed. He uses the elements of design contained in plastic forms with artistic materials – line, tone, space, colour, subject matter, and craft – to create a new and vital organism or an entity of form. He uses emotional and intellectual freedom to organise the subject or mood into a unified expression.

Indeed, creativity is like a living organism. It germinates, evolves, grows to its full height, and ends. What it leaves behind are the peaks, the high points of its development. These we term traditions or periods. There are many peaks of development, of varying heights, in a people's cultural growth as in the evolution of an artist. However, a peak is considered complete only when it has reached its zenith. Also, art like peaks, does not admit of improvement; what it admits of is its growth.

No art movement or the period of an individual artist can be an improvement on a previous stage of creation even when it has grown out of it. If authentic, it has its own ingredients, totally independent of its origin.

Admittedly art of all ages (or of periods in an individual's evolution) grows not out of itself but from the infectious virus of the creativity that preceded it. But in each period, an artist tries to create an oeuvre that reflects his immediate experience and worldview, organising it into a form that embodies the spirit of changing times, and reflects our responses to it.

Personally, in different periods and in different moods, different concerns have driven me. Some of these concerns offered relief, others stirred or provoked. The vitality of human experience needs each of these injections in varying situations. Those who make favourites of particular concerns are lovers of concerns, not of art. They get little out of this practice. Instead of becoming enriched by art, this limitation turns them into imitators of their favourites, be they artists or art lovers.

I have no favourites, either in choice of materials or

Prayer, 28" ht., granite, 2001

as regards medium. I reject specialisation as I do playing favourites. Specialisation always develops a manipulative sensibility. Being shorn of the capacity to inter-relate parts that go into the making of a synthesis, such a sensibility is prone to compartmentalised: being each part becomes a separate kingdom, denying the very unity it springs from. This, in turn, furthers man's estrangement from his environs and saps the collective will.

In a specialised society, an artist is no longer the architect nor is the architect an artist. A building is no longer a multi-dimensional creative expression. It is not something whose experience turns into an experience of ourselves. Thus, bereft of artistic nourishment, built-architecture is reduced to mere construction. The same process is repeated in the case of the architectures of painting and sculpture when they cease to absorb the vitality generated by built-architecture in its pure form.

In its truest form, architecture is an

expression of the emotional thrust of a society. As an articulation of space, it is easier for architecture to eliminate that element of remoteness that is attached to other moods of aesthetics. Painting, sculpture, poetry, even music can be ignored but not space, not building. Architectural projects embody a mental process which is repeated in the mind of each person who sees and experiences them. It offers man a way to have a total aesthetic experience. It is said that the world we build, whether good or bad, makes us understand and remember who we are.

Like theatre, to which it is often allied, built-architecture offers total artistic experience. But unlike theatre, it guarantees a certain permanence.

Towns, buildings, and objects are

Man, 30" ht., brunt wood, 1996

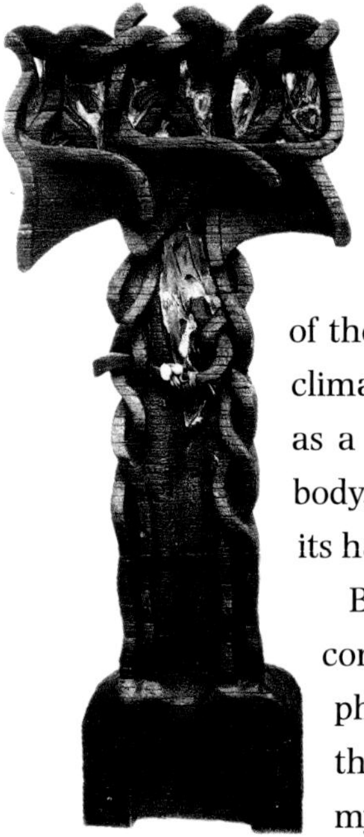

an extension of the collective memory of the individual and the community. Traditional buildings grow unconsciously out of the interaction of the landscape, soil, climate, and the material present. Just as a bird shapes its nest with its own body, a traditional community shapes its habitat with its collective memory.

Built-architecture turns a community's cosmological view into physical reality. At the same time, the temporal order is linked with the mythical order. In the end, there is complete affinity between the individual and the community, between thinking and place, between thought and feeling.

'Modern man's most urgent need,' says Edingar, 'is to discover the symbolic life and it is

Christ, 2½' ht., brunt wood, 1996

the task of the arts of space, painting, sculpture, and architecture to transfer his symbolic life into material and spatial forms.' The separation of built-architecture from the architecture of painting was a negation of this potentiality.

Painting, sculpture, and architecture are the equal manifestations of a single aesthetic. Determined by the force of necessity, all three are locked together in a common structural framework, of measure and proportion, system of movement, and echo. Thanks to this homogeneity, the dream of achieving a synthesis of the three is almost as old as their isolation from each other.

Such a need has been felt with increasing intensity, as architecture – the medium from which other art forms are supposed to derive their life and strength – continues to lose its artistic autonomy. It is being reduced to mere construction in the name of rationality and benefit. It is this loss of stature that creates a nostalgic yearning for a fusion of built-architecture with the architectures of painting and sculpture. The latter have not yet been drained to the same extent by our material and utilitarian culture.

Painting, sculpture, and architecture are products of a total environment – a social and cultural system with parallels in literature, music, and other arts and a relationship with the philosophy and science of a period.

Painters have always shown a fascination for built-architecture. Even when not indulging in designing built-architecture, their perception is fundamentally akin to that of architects.

A painter chooses a natural, suggestive, and focused sitting for the event he is depicting. In doing so, he has to reduce to their essentials the basic problems of experience posed by spatial and architectural phenomena.

In the language of painting, a city becomes a still life and a still life, a city. Painting thus represents the phenomenological chart of architecture.

The means by which artists, through the ages, have created the experience of place are exactly the same as those by which true architecture always achieved a sense of place in a building. In Cubism, in which the subject was finally subordinated, painting itself became architecture – a construction of images and associations.

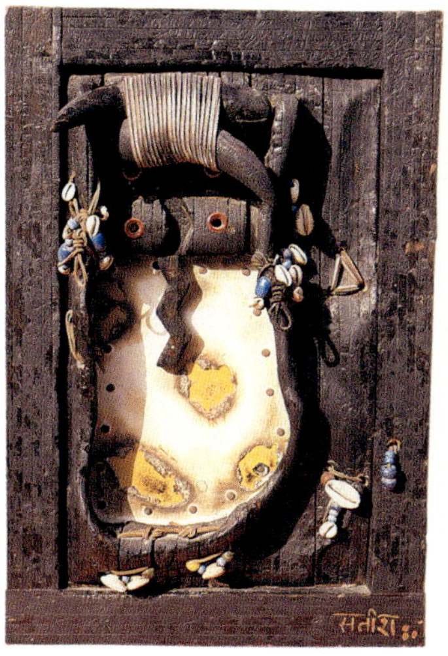

Memorial, 18" x 24", brunt wood, 1980

In my case, I was fortunate in having had my primary training at Mayo School of Arts in Lahore. Mayo was an institution where the curriculum was based on the concept of unifying the three arts, and integrating these with traditional crafts. The curriculum was the brainchild of John Lockwood Kipling, the painter-father of the legendary poet, Rudyard Kipling.

The basis of the curriculum was the belief that all three – painting, sculpture, and architecture, were arts of space. They represented an artist's attitude towards spatial organisation. They could neither exist in a vacuum, nor fully develop in isolation from each other.

The philosophy was not explained in words. Moreover this was not practical, considering the age and intellectual caliber of the students. The philosophy was rendered in graphic form. In a class supposed to teach painting, clay modeling, woodwork, stone carving, black-smithy, draftsmanship (involving scale, geometry, and perspective), and object design, were also taught.

For the simple minded, space as it is normally defined, was easy to grasp in its relationship with sculpture and architecture which are, by tradition, three-dimensional masses of volume surrounded by space. But it was difficult to comprehend this element in painting which is physically two-dimensional and possesses no projecting mass.

Kipling devised this curriculum during the late nineteenth century. The concept of using this 'deficiency' in the case of painting for finding a new category of space that was free of nature's dictates, had not yet arrived.

When I joined Mayo in the late 1930s, the same archaic method was still taught. We learnt to overcome the 'lack' of third dimensions in painting by the use of a linear and atmospheric perspective and strove to give our depictions as natural a look as possible.

Years were to pass before I was to be exposed to that new category of space which, instead of

Waiting, 24" ht., brunt wood, 2001

subscribing to the dictates of natures reduces nature's role in the creative process to a mere point of departure. Better still, I was to learn to determine my own power of transformation by the distance I would be able to keep from nature.

This new category enabled the process of creation itself to create its reality. The reality of this new architecture of painting was to be its existence. The proof of its creation was to be its being.

Space in the architecture of painting, according to this new category, was to become as much an internal experience as it was an external object. It was to become indivisible from the human condition and from man himself. It gave the artist a choice of either enlarging his self within the space or enlarging the space within himself.

Call it whatever you may: a victory of nonsense over sense, a triumph of dialectic over logic.

This is what art means to me.

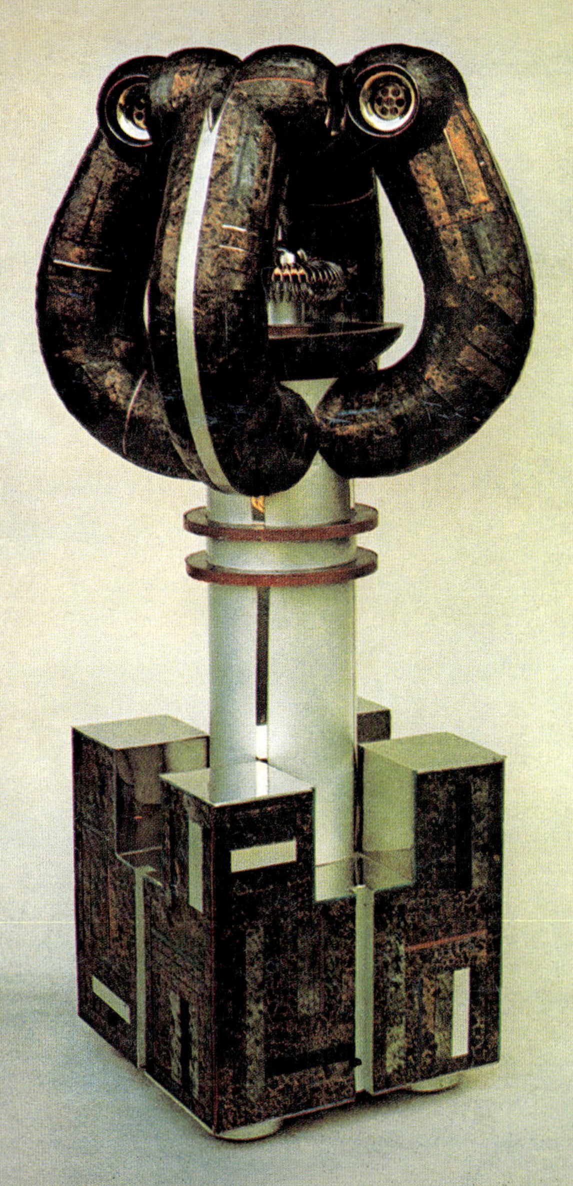

■ Nag Raj

36" ht., assorted metals, 1972

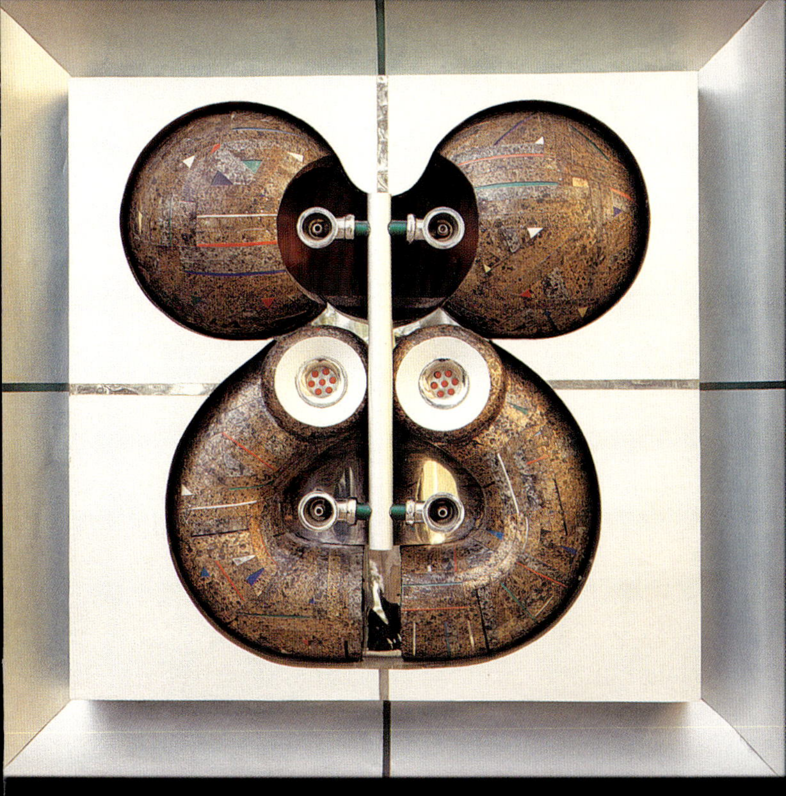

■ Laxmi

36" x 36", assorted metal relief, 1972-73

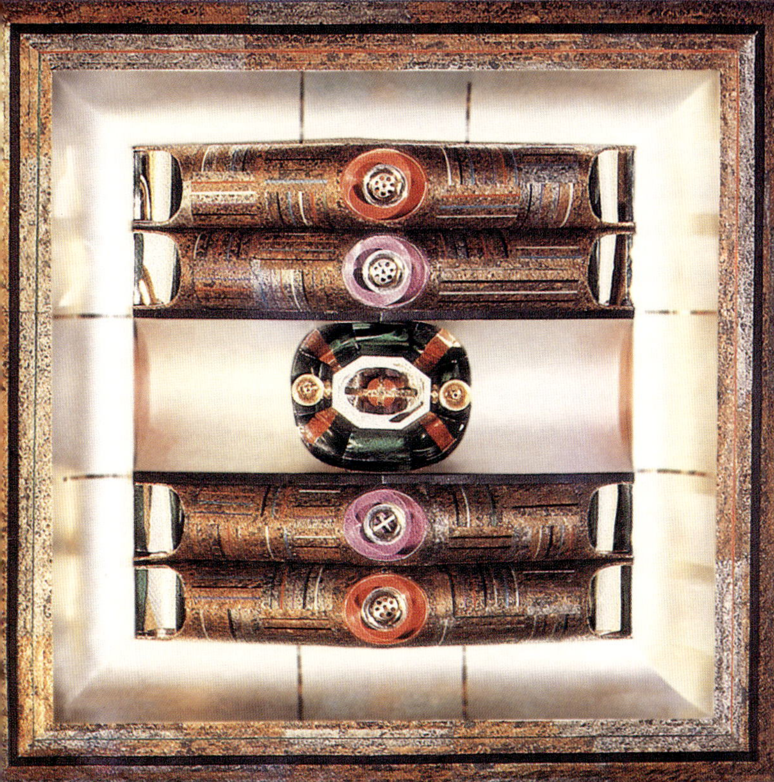

■ Tantra

36" x 36", assorted metal relief, 1973

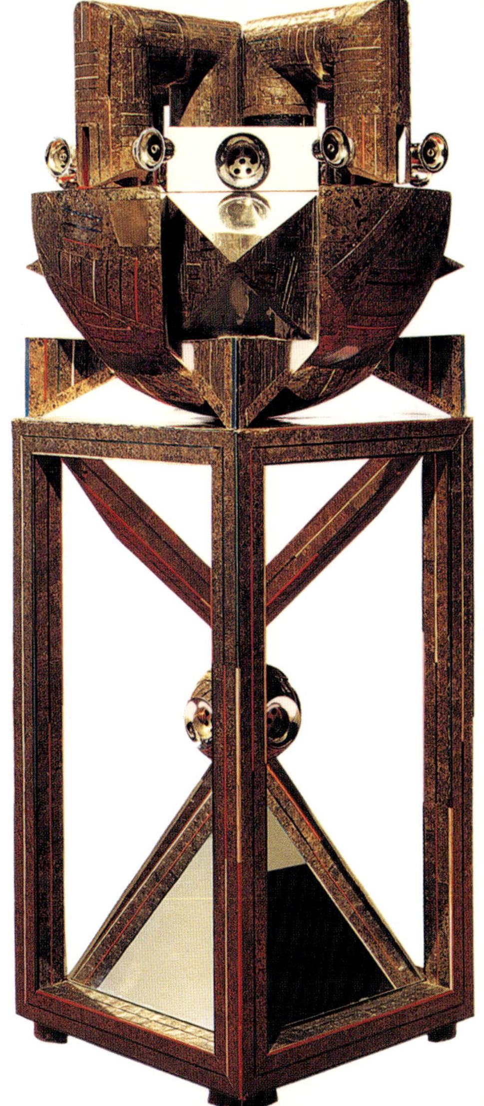

■ Ganesh

42" ht., assorted metals, 1974

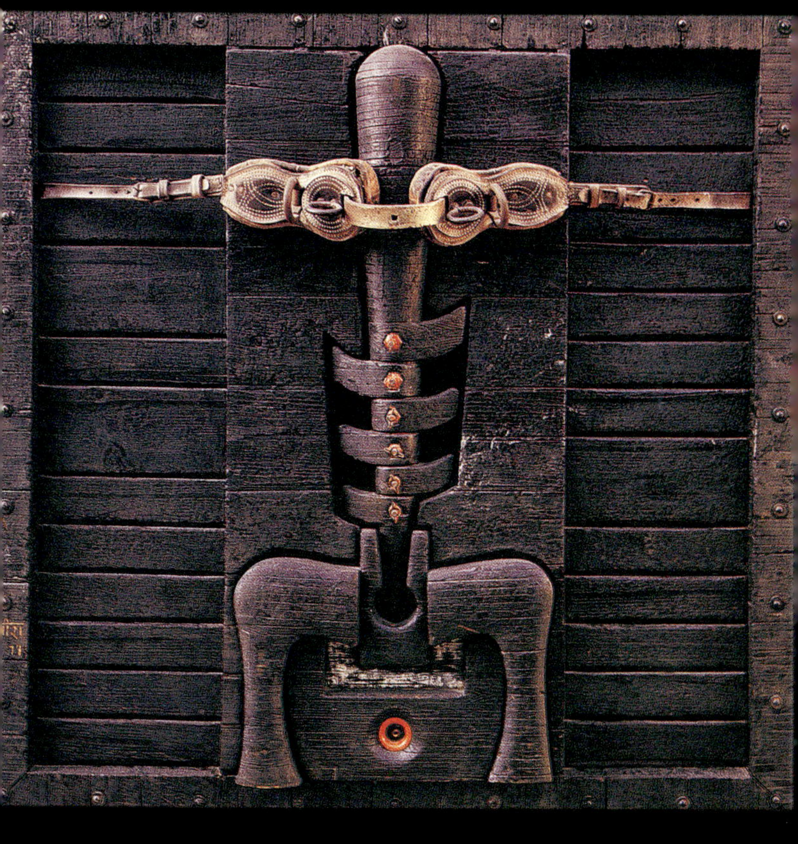

■ Crucifiction

48" x 48", brunt wood relief, 1979

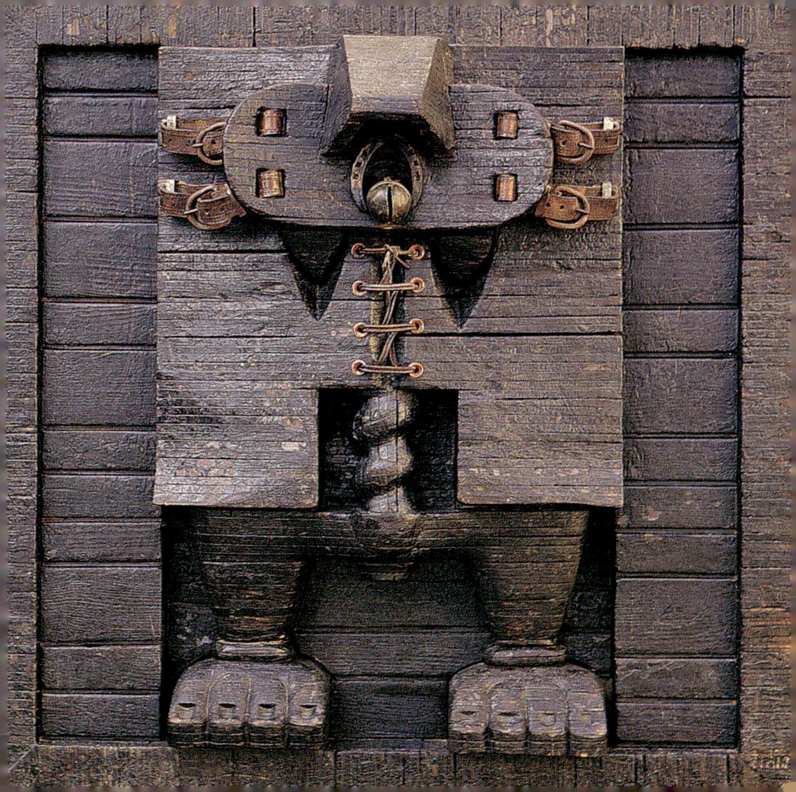

■ Shakti

48" x 48", brunt wood relief, 1978

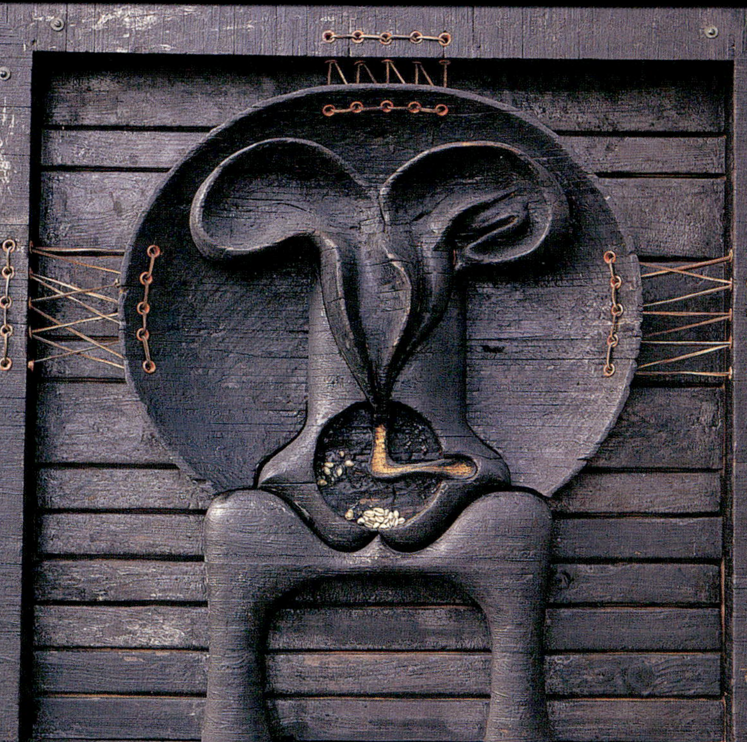

■ Ganesh

48" x 48", brunt wood relief, 1978-79

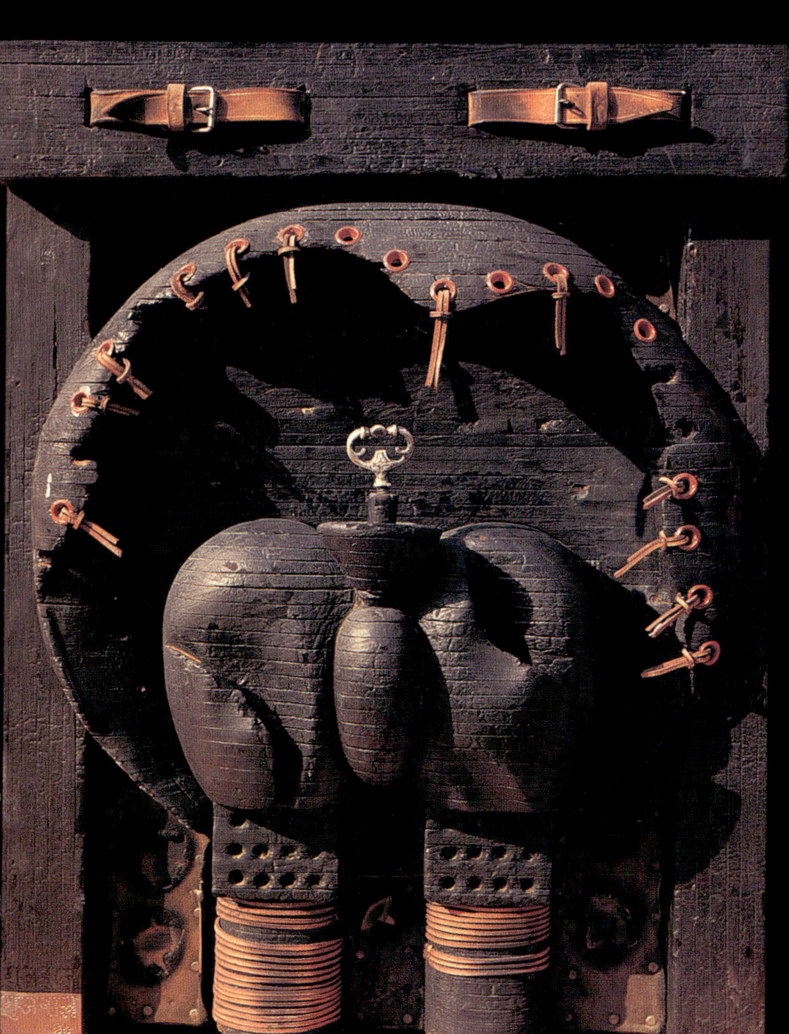

■ Nagraj

36" x 30", brunt wood relief, 1979

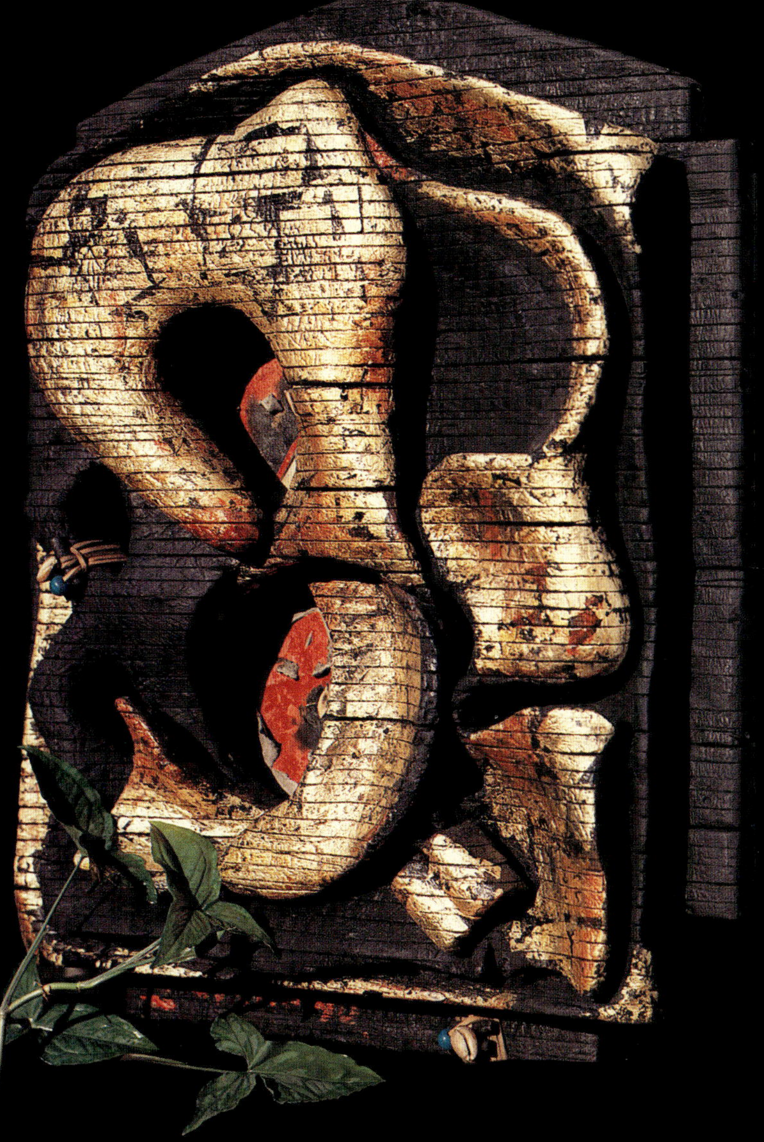

■ Ganesh

36" x 30", brunt wood relief, 1988-89

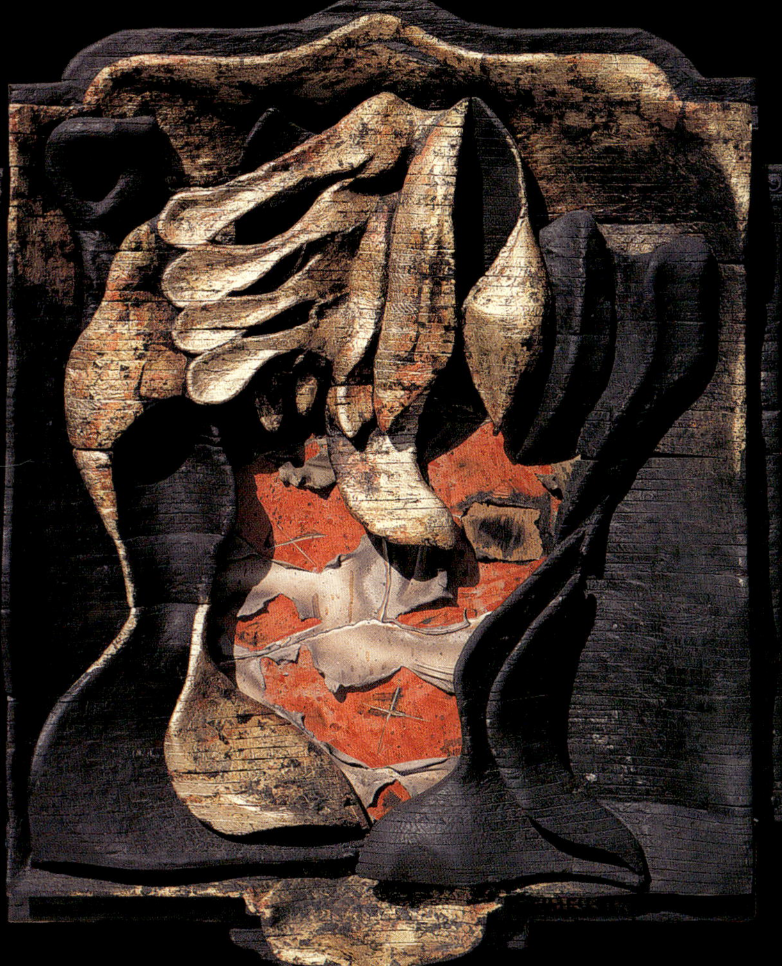

■ Deity

50" x 30", brunt wood relief, 1987

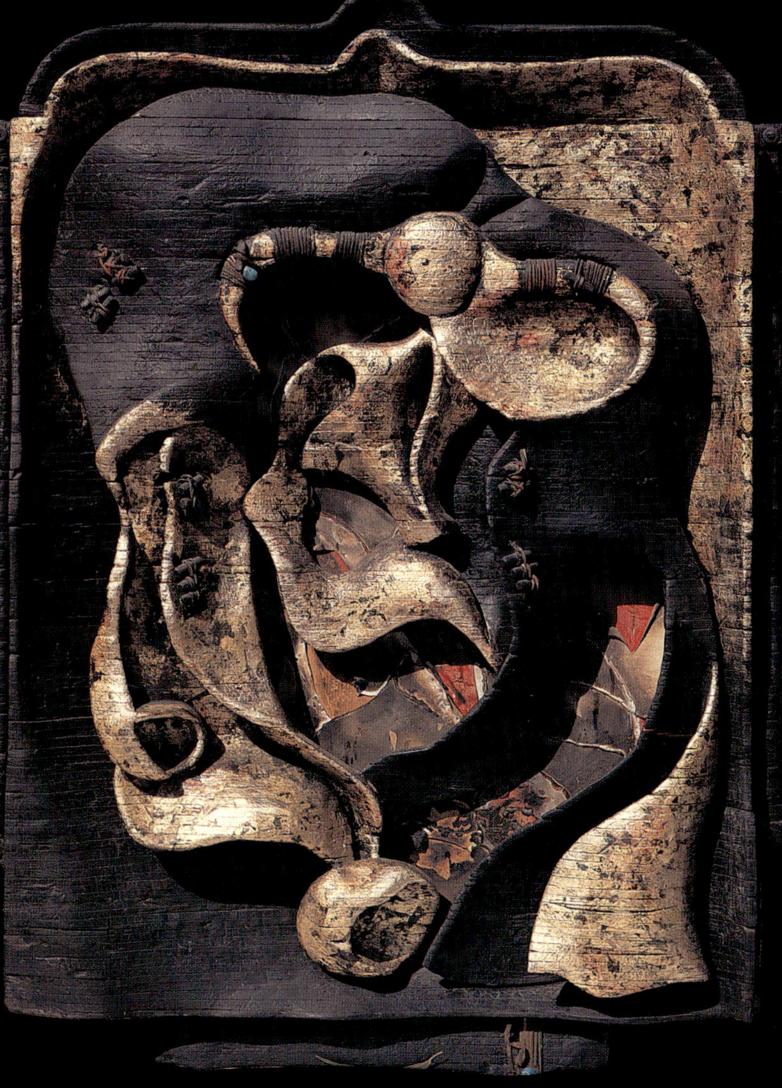

■ Birth of Ganesh

60" x 40", brunt wood relief, 1989

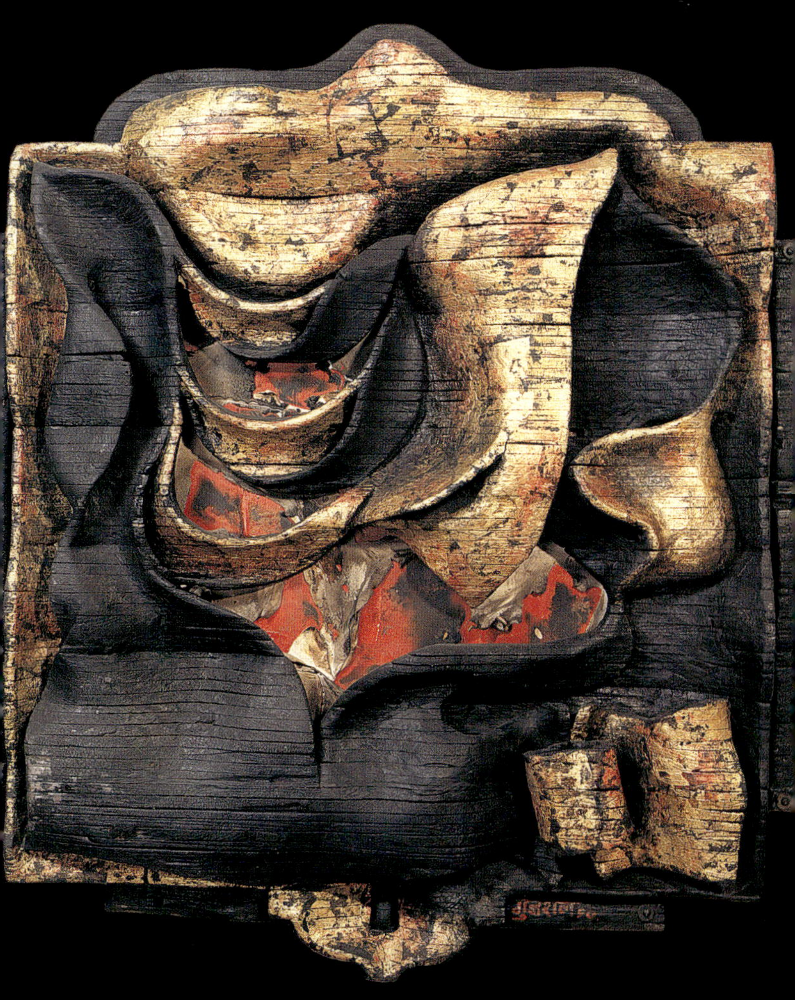

■ Deity

48" x 40", brunt wood relief, 1990

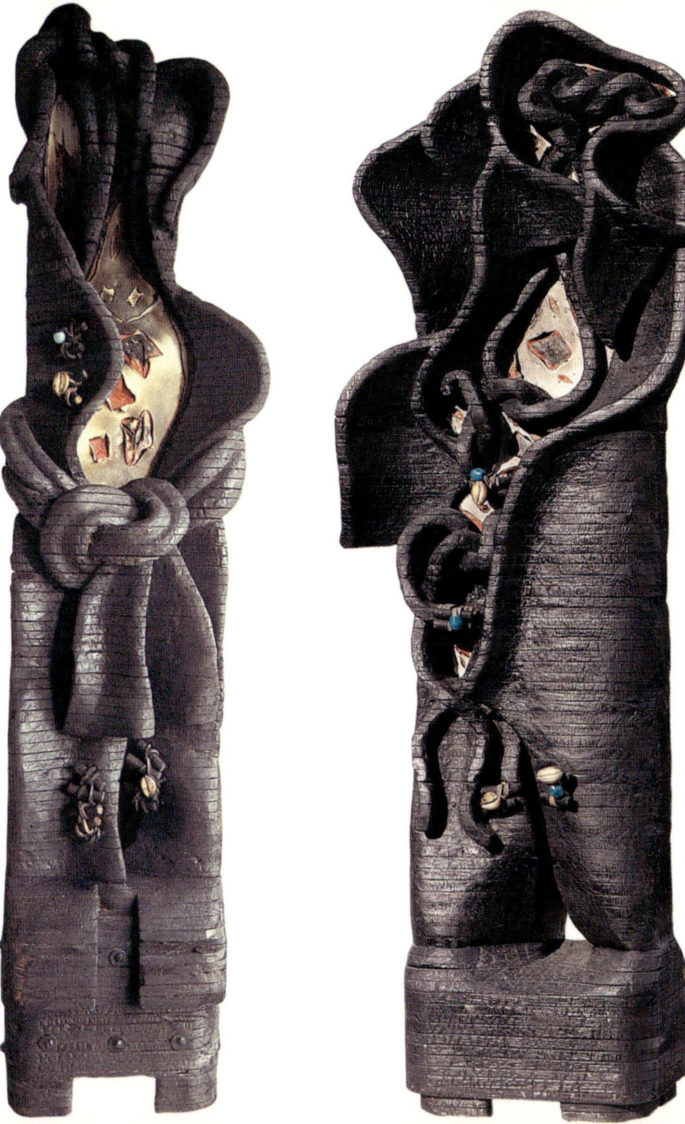

■ Woman (left), Man (right)

36" ht., brunt wood, 1991

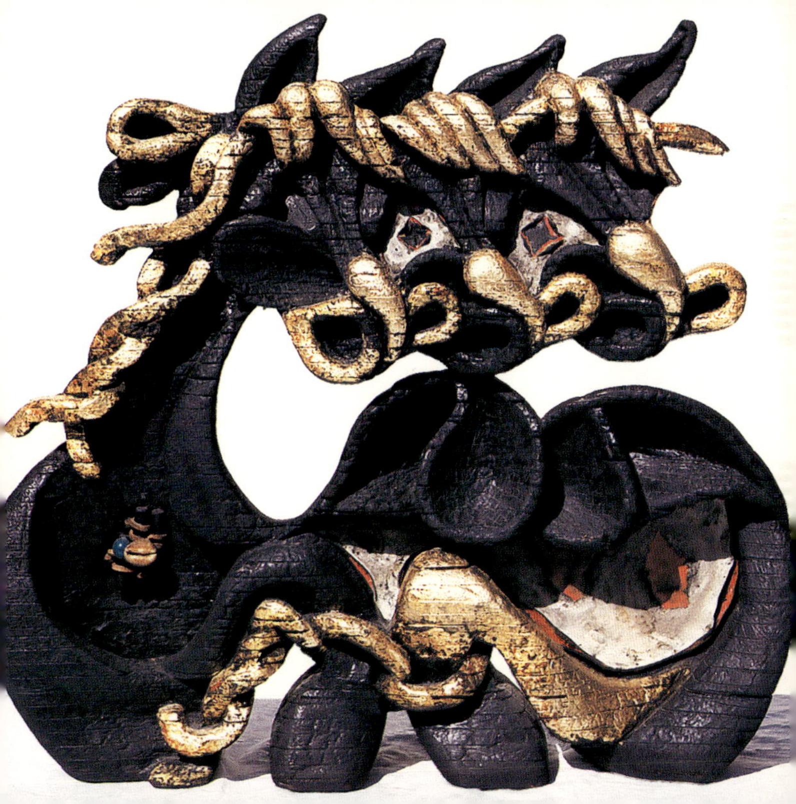

■ Horses

30″ ht., brunt wood, 1992

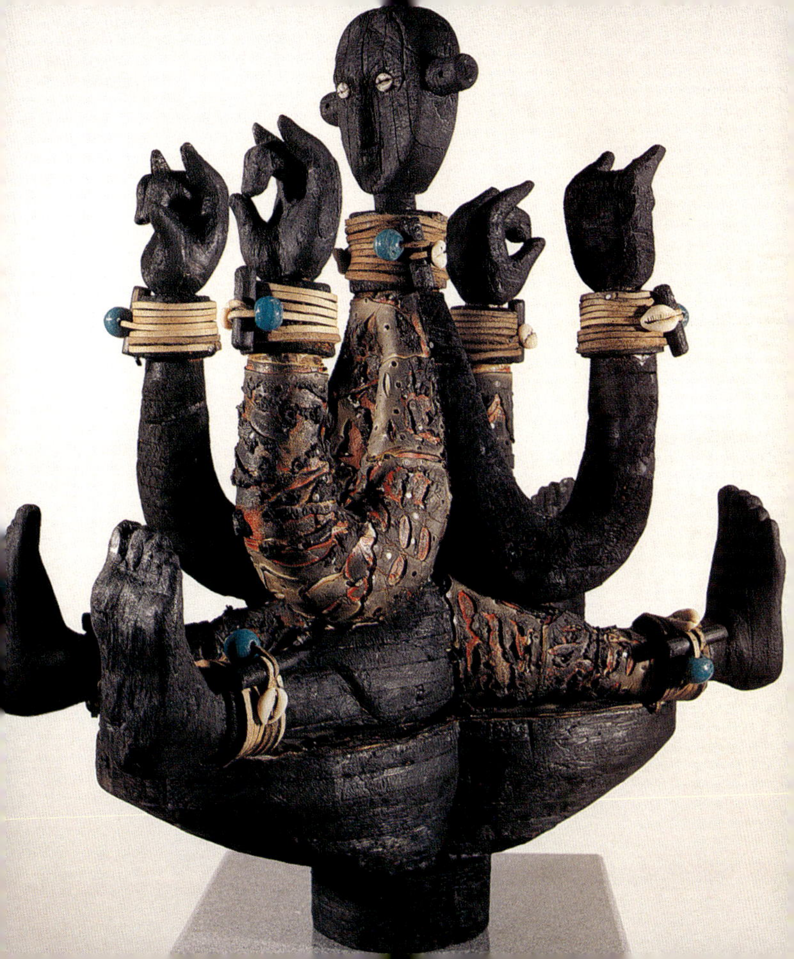

■ Shakti

30" ht., brunt wood, 2001

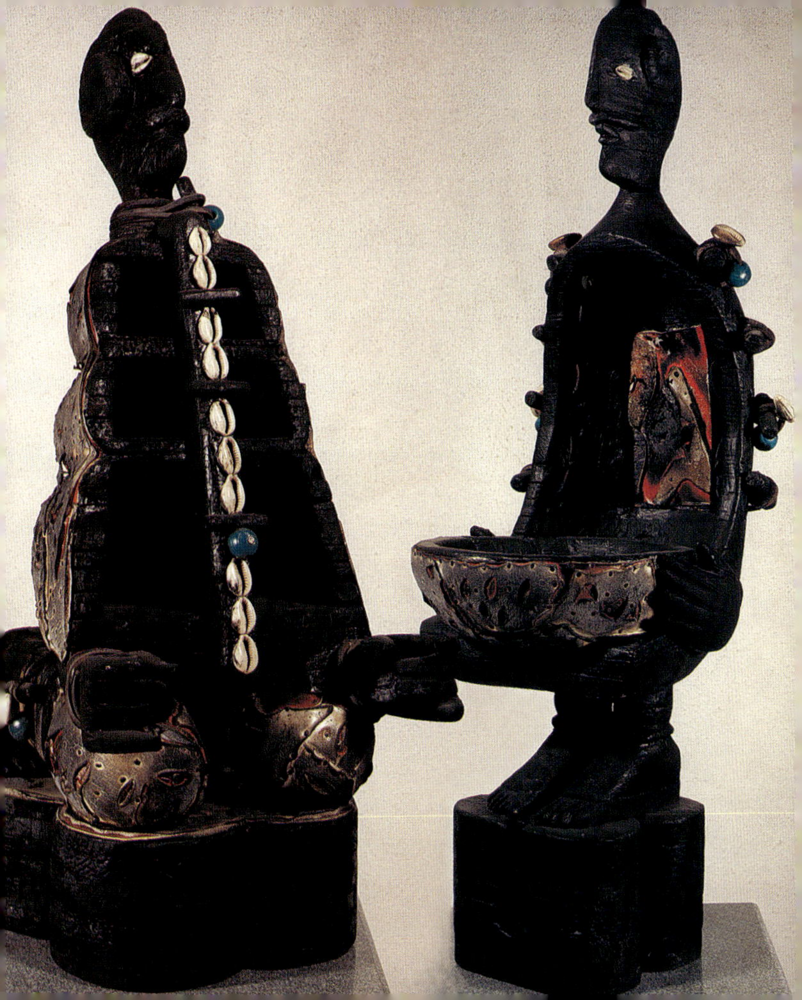

■ Invocation (left), Prayer (right)

24" ht., brunt wood, 2000

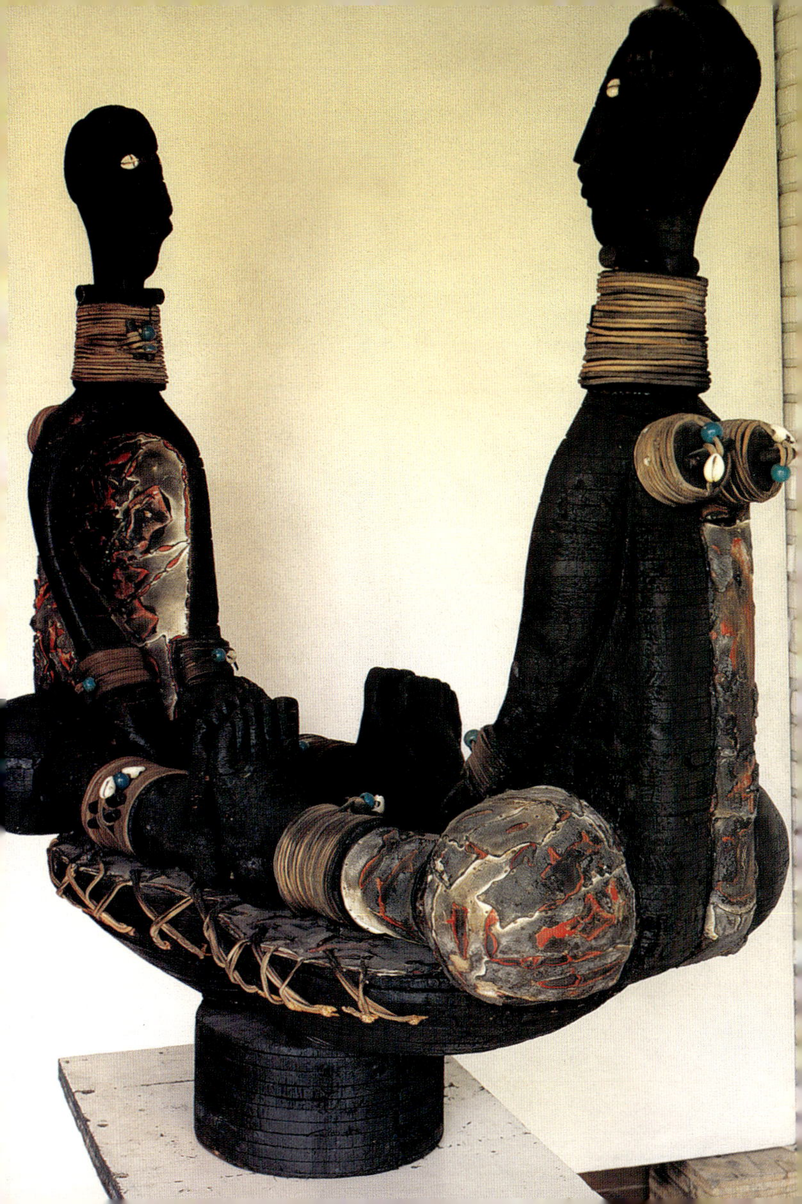

■ Gamblers

36" x 48", brunt wood, 2001

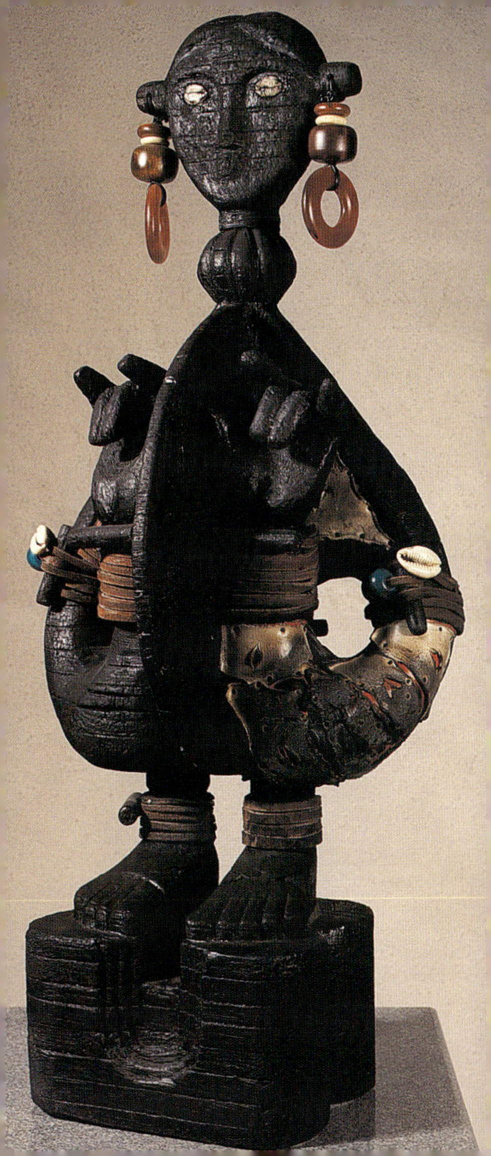

■ Laxmi

24" ht., brunt wood

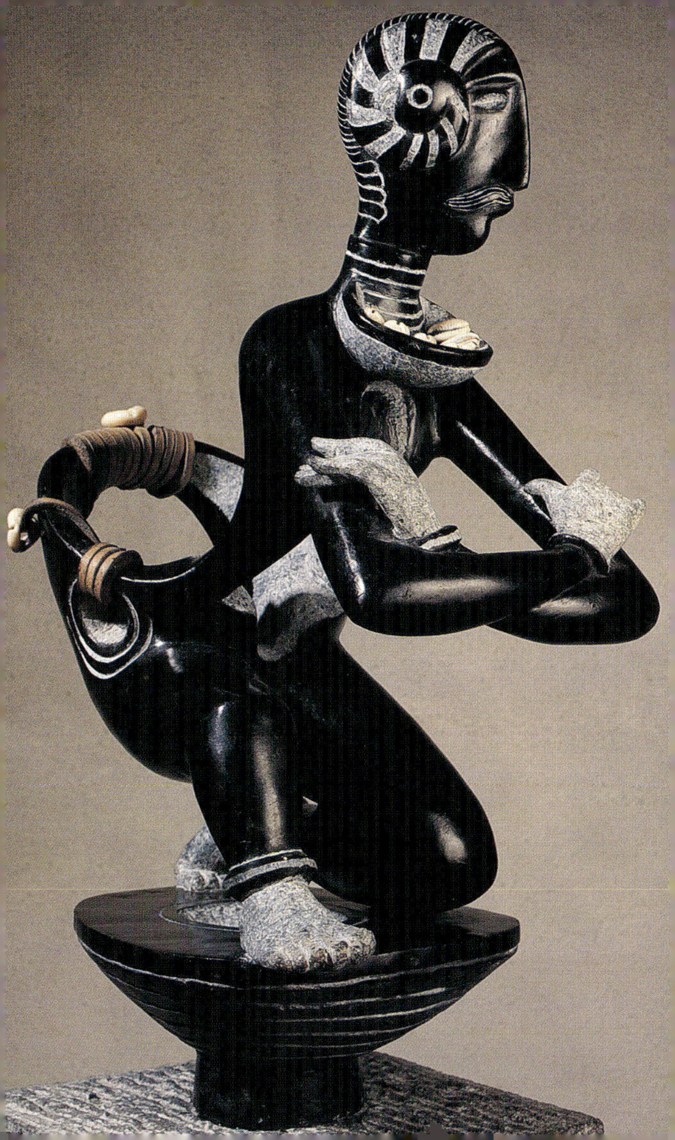

■ Wrestler

16" ht., black granite, 2001

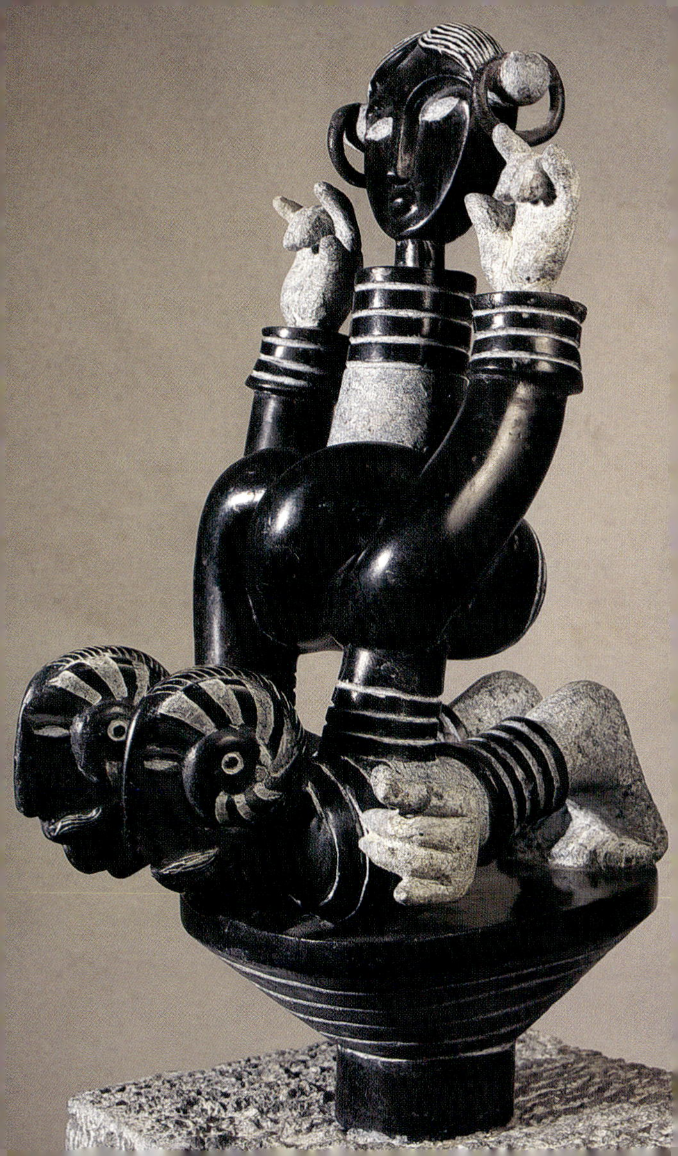

■ Kali

12" ht., black granite, 2001

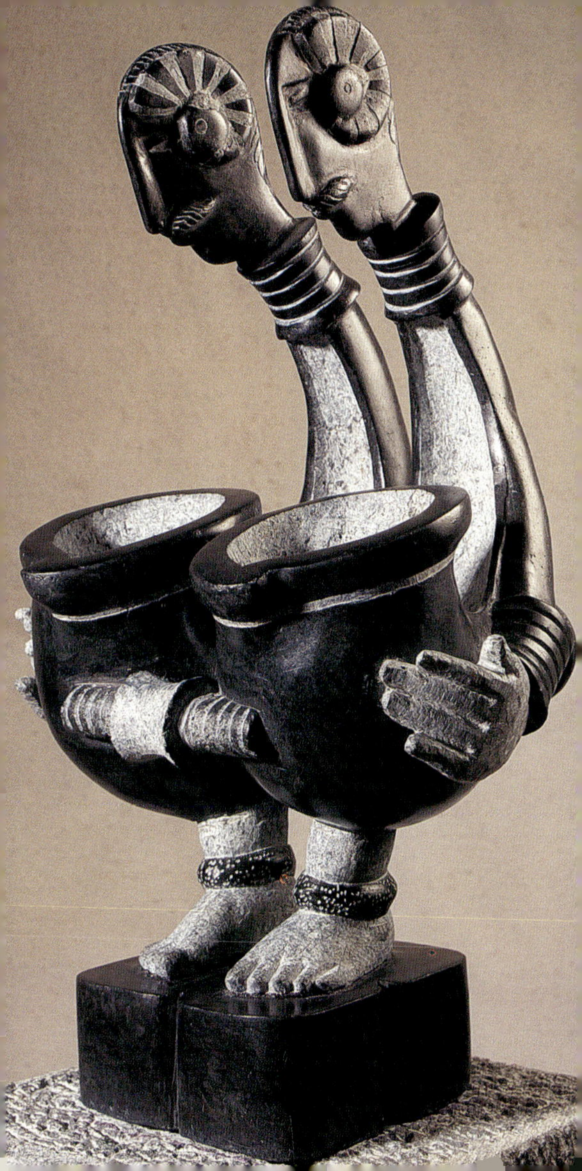

■ Drummer

14" ht., black granite, 2001

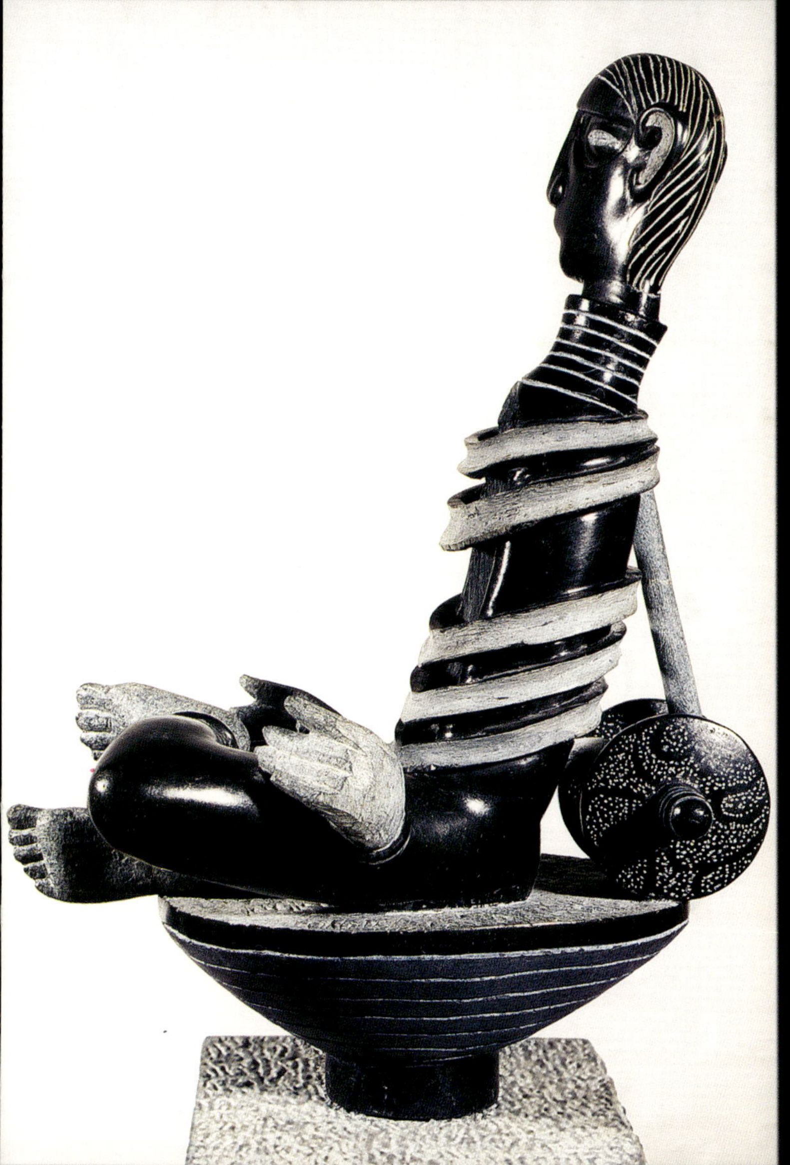

■ Expectation

14" ht., black granite, 2001

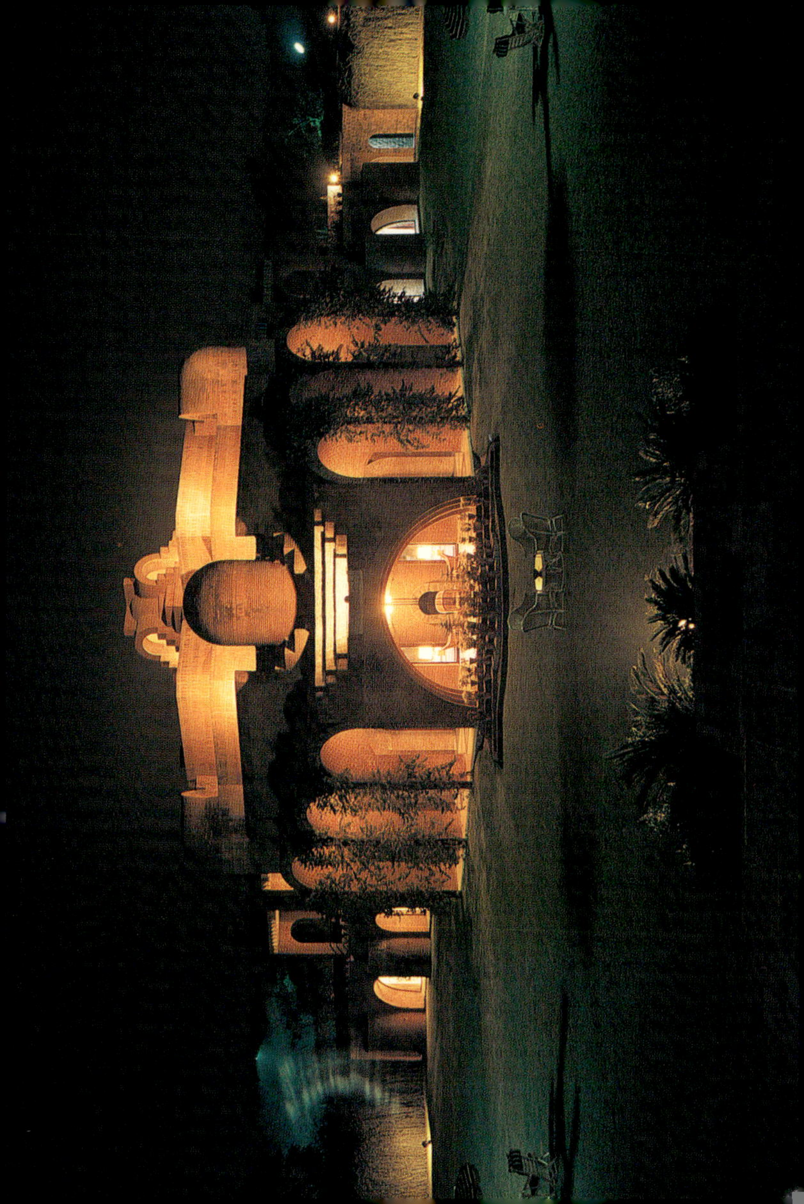

■ Belgian embassy (residence), New Delhi

1984

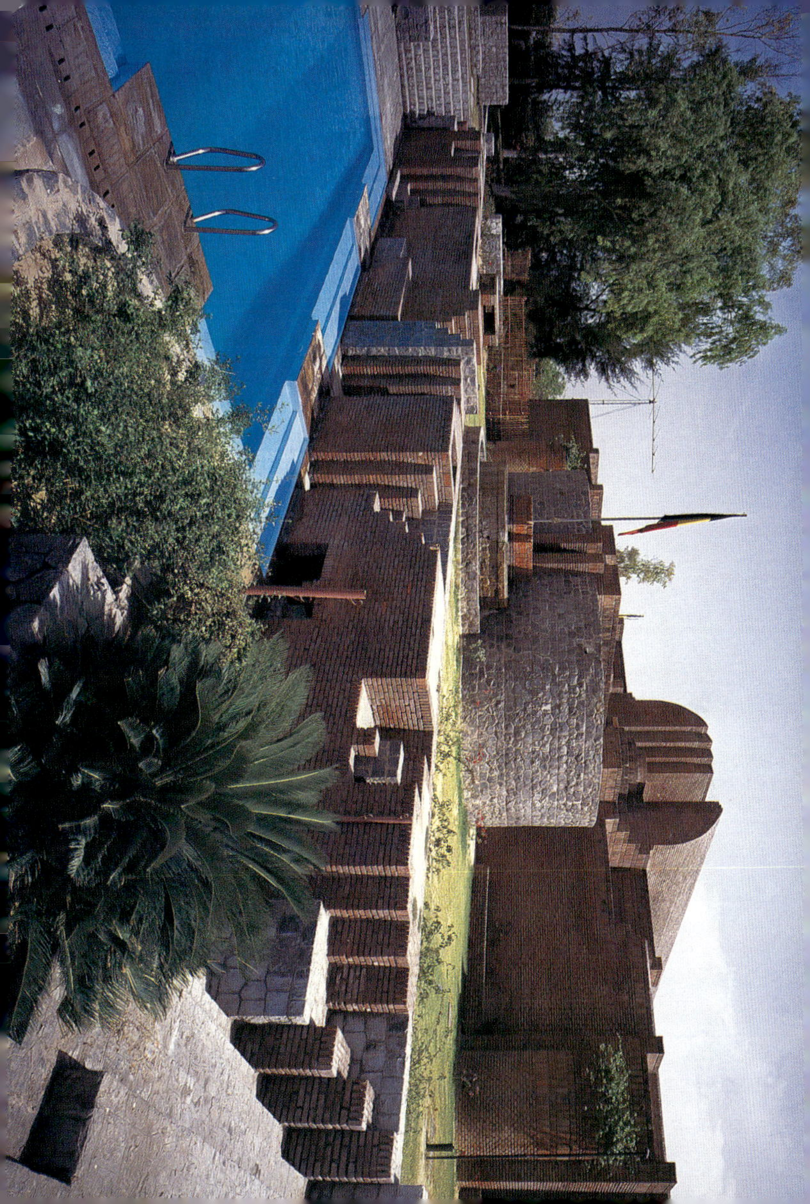

■ Belgian embassy

Swimming pool, 1984

■ *Front cover:* Invocation, 2001

■ *page 2:* Artist seated with sculptures

■ *page 3:* Unknown soldier, 1981

■ *Back cover:* Drummers, 24" ht., granite, 2001